MAKE
YOUR
MARK

MAKE YOUR MARK

The Smart Nonprofit Professional's Guide to Career Mapping for Success

NURYS HARRIGAN-PEDERSEN

NEW YORK

LONDON • NASHVILLE • MELBOURNE • VANCOUVER

Make Your Mark

The Smart Nonprofit Professional's Guide to Career Mapping for Success

Published in New York, New York, by Morgan James Publishing in partnership with Difference Press. Morgan James is a trademark of Morgan James, LLC. www.MorganJamesPublishing.com

The Morgan James Speakers Group can bring authors to your live event. For more information or to book an event visit The Morgan James Speakers Group at www.TheMorganJamesSpeakersGroup.com.

ISBN 9781683507550 paperback
ISBN 9781683507567 eBook
Library of Congress Control Number: 2017913877

Cover Design by:
Rachel Lopez

Interior Design by:
Chris Treccani
www.3dogcreative.net

In an effort to support local communities, raise awareness and funds, Morgan James Publishing donates a percentage of all book sales for the life of each book to Habitat for Humanity Peninsula and Greater Williamsburg.

Get involved today! Visit
www.MorganJamesBuilds.com

This book is dedicated to all nonprofit professionals
whose work and commitment inspire
my work, my life, and my legacy.

Table of Contents

Lost and Looking for a Map!

I t's something of the 21st century that people have career expectations beyond just a salary, benefits, title, and a place to call work. For the past few decades – and after work-life balance became a given – people have been left wanting *more*. It's no news that fewer than 50% of US employees report being satisfied at work, and this includes nonprofit organizations. In 20 years of working in staffing the nonprofit sector, I've witnessed growing dissatisfaction among nonprofit professionals despite the fact that most of them work within organizations whose mission tugs at their heart.

It happens to all of us, in many different scenarios. Let's see which one you identify with:

A job description appears and it reads exactly like what you have been looking for. This is the perfect nonprofit for you. Their mission is one that you care about and can get behind for the rest of your life. You get really excited, you tell your friends (or not if you don't want to get jinxed), and then you create the perfect cover letter to catch the attention of the hiring manager and get the call. Once the call comes in, you are polite, to the point, and positive. You schedule the interview, feeling excited and optimistic. After a few rounds of interviews with human resources, supervisors, and future co-workers, you are made a great job offer that you can't refuse. You get the job. Yes! You did it. It's your dream job! Or is it?

Months into the new role, things, both big and small that were part of the draw of the position start to annoy you. You rethink your decision briefly, but shake the thoughts away because you can't possibly go looking for a job again. You think this must be unique to you because most of your friends don't seem plagued by the same concerns. They seem happy. But you want *more*.

Or: You have been with the same organization for four years and have been promoted twice, you are doing a fairly good job most days, and the status quo is a good status quo. Compensation aligns with the market; you will most likely get another promotion in 12–18 months. You get along with your supervisor and you have great co-workers. But something is missing. You want *more*.

How did this happen? You were so clear on what you wanted to do when you grew up. Why can't you seem to get and keep a job that you love, love, love? A job that will give you that *more*?

I know what you want. You want to stop wanting. You want to fill the void, and you want to know how to do it. You know people who are doing exactly what they want to be doing and who do it well. Their lives seem easy and joyful. They are in their element, and you would consider them the ultimate professionals. Yes, they have some bad days, but that's not their norm. Bad days are the exception. They seem to have that "*more*" that you are looking for, that you crave. How did they get it? What do they know that you don't? Were they born that way? Do they have an amazing manager, or a lucky star? When you have dared ask those who seem to have a job they love, the answer is almost the same: "I knew what I wanted and I went for it." Sounds good, but how can you do that?

See, even your parents, who may have been a source of inspiration and guidance, were among those who most likely did the job at hand and didn't rattle the cage too much. They showed up at work and spent their entire life, most likely, in the same companies – or at only a handful of them. They were satisfied with having a place to work and money to care for their family.

You don't like the idea of changing jobs too often because you've been told that it doesn't look good on your resume and that you must show tenure and career progression. But tenure these days is anything beyond 18 months, and sticking it out longer than that feels hard and impractical. How are you supposed to find a job that you love if you don't keep trying different things?

Many of the professionals that I have worked with have had these same questions. They wanted *more*. Some of them found the *more*, and others didn't. What distinguished them will be revealed to you in Chapter 2. Hang in there!

Working in staffing for most of my life and exclusively for the nonprofit sector, I meet professionals who are unemployed, happily employed but want *more*, employed but unhappy, or in transition. I'm able to see first-hand how many have grappled with this issue. You are not alone in this. Most professionals all over the world want *more*. After years of hearing the same stories and the same questions; after years of seeing how many succeeded and how many others didn't; and after facing these same challenges myself, I found the *more*. I have also helped hundreds find their *more*. Following a sustainable process, I have kept the *more* in my everyday professional life. Life has never been the same.

I'm certain I know what you want:

- You want a job that you love
- You want to show up to work as your best self
- You want every day to feel like a Friday, because it feels so good!
- You yearn to have a role that is a true reflection of who you are at your core
- You want to use your true potential and hold nothing back
- You want to be authentic and not a fraud
- You want to be excited, interested, and committed to your role and your organization
- You want to be compensated for your true value
- You want to make a difference

And I want to also tell you that I know how to help you get all the things that you want. Are you ready?

As I walk you through the steps that helped hundreds of people find their *more*, I want you to leave behind all the limitations, fears, regrets, and what-ifs you have been carrying with you to this point. As I always say in my workshops, and when I work one-on-one with clients: It is never too late to create the job that you deserve and the job that brings out your Professional Identity. Did I say create? Yes, with the steps outlined in this book, you will know how to make significant and meaningful changes in the way you go about thinking of, looking for, and showing up for your dream job. These changes will help you create an empowering Career Map and will also help you embody your professional vision.

The two most common questions I am asked:

- How do I find a job that I love?
- What steps do I need to take to get there?

I consult often with nonprofits managers and leaders seeking "someone like Mary," or "someone not like John." They discuss traits that make employees "highly attractive" and "keepers." They share why a certain employee is promoted over another. I also have the employee's perspective to fill in the gaps. Many of my candidates share why certain positions bring out the best in them and why certain others have been nightmares. Over time, something has become very clear: There was a method to the madness. I started putting the puzzle together. And as fate would have it, I had to go through it myself. And then everything made sense and fell into place.

I envision a mission-driven sector with happy, fulfilled, centered professionals who are making a difference and are showing up at work fully capable and willing to share their gifts. All for the benefit of themselves, their families, their organizations, and the world.

This book will teach you how to create a unique Career Map. A Career Map is a tool that will simplify your professional path with clarity, purpose, direction, and intention.

CHAPTER ONE

My Story – Looking for the HOV Lane

For the past two decades, I have been interviewing, recommending, reference-checking, and placing professionals in all types of nonprofit organizations and positions, from data entry clerks to senior managers and leaders. I have wonderful stories to share about making the right recommendation and connecting the best professionals with the best employers and causes. I also have many not-so-great stories about professionals committing career suicide because they wanted *more* but didn't know exactly what that *more* was. So, they made poor decisions, they reacted on impulse, they left a job too early, they accepted an offer too soon, they stayed in a job for too long. They negotiated on the wrong things. They lost track of what was important.

They confused their *more* with *less*. They went for a better title, but the job didn't reflect their true potential. They went for more money, but they had less interest, excitement, and commitment than ever before. They had more responsibilities, but showed up as a far less true professional than was expected of them. They gave up so much *more* for so much less.

In my early recruiting days and in a very organic way, many of the nonprofit professionals I worked with joined me in brainstorming conversations around their career goals and aspirations. In these very casual conversations, we planned, deliberated, and found ways to materialize them.

After many years of going at it so informally but seeing all the benefits this practice provided, I decided to dedicate time and effort into turning something unstructured and unplanned into a deliberate, structured, planned, and easy-to-follow method that has changed the lives of many. I perfected a process called Career Mapping. Using this process, nonprofit professionals at different stages in their career create their unique Career Map. A Career Map is a tool that empowers nonprofit professionals to follow their dreams and pursue a nonprofit career where they can best serve and utilize their skills, experience, and unique strengths to make their mark in the world. This tool will simplify your professional path with clarity, purpose, direction, and intention.

What began as a goal-oriented process became a discovery process that I was able to share with many. I saw how successful this new and improved method was and how distinct the career outcomes were between those who followed the process and those that didn't. Professionals who created their Career Map and followed it met their career goals much, much faster and had phenomenal work experiences. Career Mapping not only provided benefits to the professional creating it, but also to the nonprofit organizations those professionals were part of or joined. It made a world of a difference. It was crystal clear to me that professionals who didn't have a plan encountered more roadblocks, obstacles, confusion, and fears that made it difficult to accomplish their career goals.

I was on a mission. Career Mapping came to life, and with it, the Professional Identity.

A Professional Identity is your true and unique professional self. It is what you are made of, your beliefs, your character, the way you decide to show up in the world and make a difference. It is made up of more than your skills and work experience. It is the true expression of your gifts and innate talents and your professional desires and aspirations. Your Professional Identity is not what you are, but who you are. Who shows up at work (excited, willing, team player, problem solver), not what type of professional role you take (Accountant, Fundraiser, Marketing Manager).

My deadly sin: I'm greedy

I always wanted *more*. More in the sense of experiences, compensation, validation, responsibilities, you name it – I wanted it. Those types of *more* changed over time. They each filled a primary need at its given stage in my life (more on those needs in Chapter 4).

Figuring out the *more* is an innate ability that I've been gifted with. I have always been fortunate in that I've enjoyed wholeheartedly all the companies I worked for, and the roles I held in those companies. And for the most part, they gave me the *more* that I craved, sometimes without many of the things that I really wanted.

Because of my own experience and exposure to thousands of professionals in the nonprofit sector and their challenges, it's easy and rewarding for me to help others find their *more* and help them create a Career Map that would get them there, without confusing the *more* with less. When I made my last professional transition from being an employee to business owner, I met with a career coach recommended by a friend to help me with some career insecurities and identify a clear path. I didn't know if I would do well as an entrepreneur or if I had what it took to start and grow a business. I wasn't sure if I was willing to leave my comfort zone and the life I'd created in NYC to chart a new personal and professional path for myself. In that moment, I became the client, not the coach. With her help, I started a career route that has taken me on journeys that are indescribable, and I have manifested all the professional dreams I'd set out for myself, with more to come. Once you create the route, the road is endless.

> *"Luck is what happens when preparation meets opportunity."*
>
> - Seneca

I plan, I prepare, and I accomplish. And so can you.

One of the main benefits for those who nurture and grow their Professional Identity within the structure of a Career Map is that they gain or regain control of the driver's seat. In my live workshops, I break the ice by asking the attendees if they use a GPS whenever they are going to a new location. The response is unanimous; they all say *yes*! Some say they use it all the time, even when they know where they are going, just to be sure!

It is the same principle with a Career Map. Professionals who have taken their time to plan and prepare accomplish *more*, and faster. More gas in their tank, more time to spare, more views to enjoy. And they experience less. Less competition, less stress, and fewer U-turns. Taking the driver's seat in your Professional Identity, and with a Career Map charting the way, changes everything. No longer are other people deciding for you. Now, you plan and act. Now, you prepare and accomplish.

Many individuals create a different identity for every job they interview for or every position they hold. What if you nurtured your Professional Identity instead and sought out a position that aligns with it? Or better yet, created a role that sustains this Identity? One of the main changes I made to get to where I wanted to be, was to connect with my Professional Identity, my true north star, and to only engage in work activities that kept it alive. Of course there will be times when you are doing work that's not in alignment, but that too should be the exception, not the norm. And if you spend most of your time in alignment with your Career Map, those times that you are not aligned will be farther and fewer in between. Why? Because you will be such an amazing contributor while in your zone of genius that neither you nor your boss will ever want to get you out of there. Yes! This is when it gets really fun. This is when you make your mark and make a real difference with the work that you do!

It is my strong belief, and I have stories to prove it, that if you feel that you are:

- in a career rut, or
- in a job from hell, or
- in career limbo,

then most likely you have not been the one making the decisions in your career. Someone else has. Even if you think that you have been, as most professionals like to believe. Most people believe they are in control, but without fail, after I do a little digging into their professional history, I help them see that they left major decisions in the hands of others. This book will help you regain control and get out of your rut, your hell, or your limbo with the help of a Career Map and the creation and release of your Professional Identity.

To give you an example of how real this concept is, from January to February 2017, Careers In Nonprofits, the staffing firm I founded in 2006 to serve the nonprofit sector, surveyed candidates in Atlanta, Chicago, and Washington, D.C., collecting 440 responses. These were the findings:

Question: Who do you think is in control of your career progression?

- **67. 08%:** I am in control of my career progression.
- **11. 06%:** I don't know.
- **7. 62%:** The executive leadership at my organization is in control of my career progression.
- **7. 62%:** The Universe is in control of my career progression.
- **6. 39%:** My direct supervisor is in control of my career progression.
- **0. 25%:** My friends are in control of my career progression.

Most people say that they are in control of their career progression, but their decisions prove otherwise. After speaking with hundreds of candidates about the career choices they've made, it is clear that a lot of weight has been given to factors outside of their true desires, intentions, and Professional Identity. There are some workplace myths that have been around for centuries that have clouded people's minds and contributed to career confusion. Myths that accuse work of being a "thief" of people's lives and dignity. Myths that distort how one should view one's career of choice and the joy of having a place to call work. How many people do you know that "work for the weekend"? Maybe you are one of them. We hear people talk about the grind and the Monday blues. Why is that? Why is it that one of the most significant sources of fulfillment in life such as having a career and making a living make so many unhappy? Shouldn't work be a source of joy and satisfaction? Why stay in a job where you are not happy or where you are not contributing at your fullest?

I believe that most people live in fear and are afraid of taking chances and taking a leap. Most people are not able to create an action plan that will catapult them to a much better position in life. They suffer at work by choice, if only by making the choice of not making changes. We give our work its meaning. And what we put in, we take out. Therefore, if we take the time to put in the right energy, set of goals, purpose, and intention into our Career Map, the results might work for us very well.

Taking responsibility and deciding to make your mark often times requires leaving the known for the unknown. I know that it was very difficult for me to leave my close group of friends and chart a new path. I had college friends and roommates with whom I'd grown into adulthood and shared a life. It was difficult to plan a future without them. But I wanted *more*. I dreamt of starting and growing my own business. I also dreamt of living in different cities around the US. When I decided to pursue a promotion with my former employer, relocate to Washington, DC, and then, shortly after that, start my journey of business ownership, I was really on my own. None of my best friends were business owners, and we couldn't relate at that level. They were all very supportive and encouraging, but we started to live different lives. I had to decide: Did I want to continue going for my dreams, or did I want to stay in my comfort zone? Making conscious, clear choices is a habit that can be learned. And it's never too late to start.

Where do you start?

You start from the beginning. If you go back to the times when you have accepted a position, most likely you sought out the opportunity, applied, interviewed, and voilá, you had a job offer in front of you. They wanted you. That is very flattering! An employment offer is exciting especially if you have been unhappy or unemployed for some time.

But now, you are in reacting mode. You see, without a Career Map that outlines where exactly you want to be two or five years from now, it is very easy to lose track of what your Professional Identity really wants or needs to flourish. Now, you are being and doing what your employer wants you to be or do, and not your authentic self. The majority of organizations are not in the habit of taking the time to help you figure out what your next career moves are going to be and the purpose behind those moves. They don't do it intentionally; it's not to keep you unhappy. It's just not a common practice. It's kind of a "don't ask, don't tell" unwritten policy. You are told when the promotion is effective and when you will get a raise. These key decisions are made for you and with little of your input.

The goal of my private sessions, this book, and my workshops is to empower you to be an active part – if not the lead – on all this key decision-making. With a Career Map, you are a full participant and you will honor your employer and organization with the best expression of your Professional Identity. Only when you are an engaged and an aware dancer in this dance can you use your full potential and all your amazing gifts to contribute at a higher level.

SMART goals

SMART goals have been around since the 19th century. It is still unclear who first came up with the concept. Becoming very good at creating and setting SMART goals is a pivotal part of the Career Mapping process. They keep you accountable and on track in getting to your destination. The ride as well as the end point should be full of fun experiences, satisfaction, and fulfillment.

SMART goals are:

- **Specific:** Not vague. Exactly what do you want?
- **Measurable:** Goals should be quantified. How will you know if you've achieved it or not?
- **Attainable:** Being honest with yourself about what you can reasonably accomplish at this point in your career, while taking into consideration your current responsibilities.
- **Realistic:** It's got to be doable, real, and practical.
- **Time-based:** Associate a time frame with each goal. When should you complete the goal?

As you create your Career Map, you will set goals for yourself in the form of assignments and action items. You will also apply the SMART test to see if they are as strong as they should or can be. I strongly believe that goals are the stepping stone to career success. As you go for growth and expansion, you will set yourself up for success by being diligent, creative, and getting out of your comfort zone.

Let's jump to the second chapter. Your roadmap to success awaits!

CHAPTER TWO

Why a Career Map?

As I prepared to switch into the unknown world of business ownership, one thing I knew for sure was that those professionals I worked closely with had a much better ride, transition, and arrival once they had planned their course. I wanted to do the same. I wanted to use a guide that would get me there the quickest and with the most guaranteed success. I wanted to take calculated risks and make smart moves while being true to myself, my Professional Identity, abilities, and dreams. The next logical step was to create my own unique Career Map, and, with the help of my career coach, I embarked on the journey. My unique Career Map was very specific about my end goal, the steps I needed to take to get there, and the SMART goals I needed to meet along the way.

After creating a great transition (yes, I did it!) with enormous professional gratification and success, I was even more convinced of the value and power of a Career Map, and made it a personal and professional commitment to create a movement around Career Mapping and to promote its benefits and values to professionals in the nonprofit sector. I earnestly set out to produce a five-step process centered on Career Mapping. This process is meant to give you a simple and guided route to help you surface out of career limbo or career rut, or to make a career transition. A transition in which you are fully aware and conscious of every step and where you are empowered the entire time. A Career Map, created by you, gets you to where you want to be. Irrelevant of what the job boards say, the job indexes say, and the news say. Irrelevant of what promotions are offered and what job offers you have on the table. You start in the driver's seat and remain in the driver's seat until your choose not to be.

As you embark in this joyous, sometimes terrifying, and always rewarding process, I want you to choose your level of participation. You will get out of it what you put in. And if you stick with it, I promise you will have everything you need for professional and personal fulfillment. At the end of this five-step process, it is my goal that you have a beautiful, compelling, and exciting Career Map. These are the steps:

Step 1: Achieve Clarity
Step 2: Find Purpose
Step 3: Set Direction
Step 4: Gain Intention
Step 5: Prepare for Obstacles

It'd like to reiterate that it is essential to dive deep into introspection and to be brutally honest with yourself during this process. In fact, this process will only work for you if and when you engage with total authenticity; it's the most important requirement. Having a Career Map on hand, designed and brought to life by you, will propel you forward with confidence, clarity, and a strong sense of who you really are, what you really want, and how you will get there. Once you embody your authentic Professional Identity, it will be easy for the world, prospective employers, and current managers to see. In Chapter One, I described your Professional Identity as your unique set of talents, experience, desires, and interests. I also described your Professional Identity as not *what* you are, but *who* you are. It's who and how you show up at work – excited, willing, eager to be a team player, engaged in problem-solving – not what your job title says you are – accountant, fundraiser, marketing manager.

With a Career Map you can get:

- More of the work you are destined to do
- More enjoyment of your 9-5
- More enjoyment of your personal time outside of work
- More satisfaction and pride in your results
- More gratifying work experiences
- More clarity, purpose, direction, and intention
- More alignment with the people you report to and supervise
- More compensation
- More ease in accomplishing professional and personal goals
- More opportunities that you align with

I'll share with you two case studies of nonprofit professionals I had the joy of seeing go from job limbo to career success. Linda attended one of my Career Mapping workshops and, after working diligently on the five-step process, she experienced a complete professional shift. Linda gained clarity and outlined steps to follow to get her where she wanted to be. As a Director of Development at a midsize nonprofit organization, she was unsure if she wanted to continue going up the ladder to eventually became an Executive Director or if she wanted to do something different. She had some beliefs, assumptions, and professional needs that were paralyzing her. However, after gaining clarity she knew that her Professional Identity would not thrive as an Executive Director, even though it was expected of her by her peers, society, family, and herself. Her Professional Identity was truly happier serving in a different capacity. She wanted to remain in fundraising, and she decided to do so. Not from a place of fear. Not because she was afraid to fail as an Executive Director, but from a place of strength. From a place of knowing exactly what and who she wanted to be. What her gifts to the world were and in what space she could better share them.

And then there was Daniel. Relatively new to his career, he held different positions at two very different types of nonprofits. He liked them both. But he wanted *more*. He couldn't point out what the *more* was; he was insecure about making any choices or taking any steps. After gaining clarity and answering some tough questions, he came to the realization that although he had the skills, experience, and personality to manage a team, his lack of confidence and trust in himself was holding him back. He felt that he had been scattered and unfocused, and didn't have much of a track record to show. Career Mapping outlined the steps he needed to take and the gaps he needed to close to make his professional *and* personal dreams come true. He was able to build his confidence and shortly after was managing a small team. Daniel was making his mark!

You see, this proven method of helping you gain clarity, purpose, direction, and intention in your professional life will inevitably affect your personal life as well. Once you follow the steps outlined, you will have the tools you need to thrive and make positive changes. Diligently working each step and participating intently will make the process smooth, efficient and enjoyable. Take ownership of the process, it's all about the fact that YOU are the one doing it this time around. These are not new concepts, it is because once you take on the challenge to jump into the driver's seat, life changes and it will never be the same again. You will embark on a journey where you will accomplish your dreams and create new ones. You will change your route as needed and be in total control the entire time.

One of my biggest satisfactions is seeing, from the very first exercise, how many of my clients start connecting the dots and gaining confidence, even while taking baby steps. Call it divine inspiration, magical intervention, or simply coming to terms with what is. Whatever you choose to call it, know that the breakthroughs will follow. With your focus and participation this process unfailingly moves you from point A to point B. Your career rut or limbo will be a thing of the past. And shortly, you will arrive at career bliss – for sure! I've seen it time and time again.

At Career In Nonprofits (CNP), we run an internal workshop where all staff members create their own Career Maps. This usually elicits two different outcomes from my staff: I either see increased loyalty and commitment, or I see resignations on my desk. This process is very eye-opening. There was a period of time where I didn't want to lose staff and was not offering the workshop. But at the end of the day, those people who were going to leave, left anyway. Career Mapping was just a catalyst to making the inevitable departure happen a bit sooner. Now I realize that this, too, was a blessing in disguise. There is no point in holding on to employees who are not committed. On the other hand, those whose Career Mapping and Professional Identities aligned with the organization's vision and mission have created incredible trajectories for themselves within the organization.

One of our team members, Sara, was apprehensive to share with me that it became very clear to her that although she loved working at Career In Nonprofits, her Career Map confirmed that ultimately she wanted to move to a warmer city (she was working at our Chicago branch at the time). Coincidentally, our company's five-year business plan included expanding our territory to Atlanta, so we were able to keep Sara on board and happy. But it could have gone the other way, and here is where it can get scary. But you can't let fear hold you back from being loyal to your Professional Identity and finding yourself in the job of your dreams. Imagine all the possibilities if you were to operate from a place of strength and not from a place of fear! Sara and I both won. With Career Mapping, there is always a win-win.

Going through the Career Mapping process will help you confront your fears – or at the very least help you identify them and move forward in spite of them. The five-step process will also reduce the risk of you committing some of the mistakes that most professionals make:

- Applying for jobs that they qualify for but don't really want
- Applying for jobs that they really want but are not qualified for
- Staying in positions where their Professional Identity is absent
- Seeking promotions because it is what's expected of them
- Seeking salary increases without strong justification

- Not leaving dead end jobs early enough
- Staying in roles where they are unhappy for too long
- Accepting job offers too quickly
- Grieving a job that they lost for too long
- Obsessing over the wrong things
- Believing that their career success is in the hands of someone else

Working deliberately on your clarity, purpose, direction, and intention and preparing yourself to overcome obstacles will help you create your unique Career Map and release your Professional Identity, which in turn will become your GPS, your guiding compass. I highly recommend working on your chapter exercises with pen and paper. Buy a colorful notebook and make it your Career Mapping journal, or create one as a Word document – but don't try work on it all in your head. Your commitment and re-commitment will be needed!

As you confront your fears and start exploring the edge of your comfort zone, I highly recommend that you shift your mindset and approach Career Mapping from an empowered state. Let go of all those things that have not worked for you and get into the core of your emotions, your values, and your priorities at this stage of your life. Career Mapping is a tool. This tool is the key to unlocking your Professional Identity and always operating from that place. Once you find it, all the things that you have been longing for in a job, field, or career will materialize with ease. And it will be authentic. It will be yours.

Starting from an empowered state will ensure that the decisions around your Career Map will serve you at the highest purpose. It will also serve those touched by your work at the highest level. When you start with the right frame of mind, free of limiting beliefs and fears, you are able to operate from the conviction that your Professional Identity will make the right choices.

How do you quiet the outside voices and let your Professional Identity speak? By asking yourself the right questions, questions that will uncover the hidden obstacles in the way of becoming the professional that you yearn and are meant to become. Only from a centered, focused, determined, and positive place can you discover what is missing and create meaningful steps to take. Operating from a frustrated, fearful, doubtful, and unclear space will result in more of the same. You have to clear the space for wonderful things to happen.

To have a good sense of where you are right now in terms of skills and experience, please take some time to take a **Professional Inventory**. The skills and experience listed on the chart can easily be replaced with those in the position that you are trying to grow into or transition to. Jump into this exercise with both feet and strip your answers from concepts like what you "should be" or have been told that you are. This is a true inventory that reflects vital parts of your Professional Identity.

Professional & Personal Inventory

Please go through the following checklist and rate each skill as a strength or weakness. If you've rated it as a weakness, develop a proactive plan for addressing this weakness. Be honest with yourself. With brutal honesty, please rate your skills and experience in the following areas on a scale of 1-5, 5 being the highest. Anything rated 3 or less is considered a weakness.

Professional And Personal Inventory

With brutal honesty, please rate your skills and experience in the following areas on a scale of 1-5, 5 being the highest. Anything rated 3 or less is considered a weakness.

Professional Skills/Experience	Score	List 3 Ways In Which You Will Address This Weakness
Management of Small Staff		
Management of Large Staff		
Accounting/Finance		
Fundraising		
Human Resources		
Technology		
Program Development		
Personalize		
Personalize		
Related Education Required		
Other		
Personal Skills/Assets		
Ability to Focus on Task at Hand		
Ability to complete work on a Timely Manner		
Ability to Manage Difficult Situations		
Ability to Manage Work/Life Balance		
Ability to work Alone or With a Team		
Flexibility		
Self Confidence		
Health		
Personal Development		

CHAPTER THREE

Gaining Clarity

You are going to end up someplace, but where? You are going to become someone, but who?

When it comes to your career and professional development, taking control of the course, planning, and outcomes of your Career Map will give you a sense of accomplishment like nothing else. Once you are in control and functioning in your Professional Identity, the outcomes will align with who you are and with your desires. Your presentation to the world will be genuine. I've seen firsthand how successful professionals have made a dramatic turn for the better once they are in the driver's seat with a clear vision of the road, a map in hand, and a compass.

Clarity must lead the way. You may be confused about the direction that you want to go, or you may know exactly where you want to end up, but don't have a clue of how to get there. You may know the steps needed to get there but may lack confidence and direction. These are all scenarios that are very common among professionals at all levels and fields in the nonprofit sector, and in fact are more common than not. I've been in all three of those scenarios at different times in my life. Be assured that you can make changes, and that this is not how it is supposed to be. That's a myth. Being clear about where you want to go and how to get there, with confidence and trust in your decision-making, is what makes your unique Career Map effective for you.

The first step in the process of Career Mapping is obtaining clarity about your destination. Getting clear on what you really want can be a confusing and frustrating process. And at the same time, it can be very empowering – the kind of power you need to regain control of the driver's seat. Most people daydream about a better work situation, one where they may have a different title, make more money, or have a better commute. But the grass is not always greener on the other side, and I invite you to consider long and hard what your heart desires before making any decisions around your career goals. Gaining clarity will make this part of the ride so much smoother. I recommend spending time thinking about the type of professional experiences you are after. This is not related to specifically the "job" itself, but the life experiences in the work place that you are looking to gain.

As you seek clarity, a great place to start is by asking yourself who you want to be in your new role. Not the job title, but who that person is who is going to show up at the interview, on the first day at work, and for every day thereafter. Then, in the context of that, consider the role you'll play in the organization and if it's in alignment with your Professional Identity.

- How will you show up (energized, guarded, open)?
- What role will you play (team player, leader, innovator)?
- Is your Professional Identity engaged (will you be operating in full gear or neutral)?

How will you show up?

People who are doing work that matters to themselves and others always show up. They show up to the interview knowing exactly what skills, experience, and willingness to succeed they bring to the table. They are certain about their interest level. They also know how they will make their mark once they are in the position. Gaining clarity before you make a career move avoids U-turns. As you create your Career Map, be conscious of lies that you've been told by others and that you've told yourself that might taint your clarity:

- "You are too smart for that job."
- "Nobody loves their job."
- "You are asking for too much money."
- "You are not meant to be happy at work, that's why is called work."
- "I can never compete with smarter people."
- "I need to leave this role to grow."
- "I shouldn't rattle the cage too much, or I will lose."

These are lies that you may have believed in order to stay in your comfort zone. They have served you until now, but in your quest to create your unique Career Map, you must let them go, and go deep to discover what your truth is.

I invite you to question your beliefs about who you are. Will you show up as successful or defeated? Will you show up knowing what you believe is true about you? When looking for a new position, professionals with a powerful and unique Career Map know exactly what beliefs about themselves and the world they have. They know what makes them jump out of bed every morning ready for the day and what they stand for.

Once you stand crystal clear on this, it will be so much easier for others to see. Your light will shine bright. Choose who you want to be. And work toward creating that person.

What role will you play?

Happy and inspired nonprofit professionals are certain of the professional assets they bring to the table. If it's accounting, let's say, they are able to confidently articulate in what area of accounting they can make the biggest contributions, which one of their many skills is their strongest, and what type of duties they would like to stay away from because those duties are far from their zone of genius. They have clarity on all these key points *before* they even apply to a new job. They are not afraid to be transparent during the interview process and ask the many questions they need to ask to help them decide if this role aligns with their Career Map, Professional Identity, and the role they've have chosen to play. Confidently choose those things you want to do and create goals around making it happen.

Who you want to be and what you want to do are two completely different things, and being clear on each is essential. You may want to be a happy, innovative, and creative Marketing Manager. Or a reserved, polite, and enigmatic Director of Programs. Choose! You are in control. Whether you are doing it consciously or not, you are choosing the role you've been playing. Which one is it? Is it a favorable one? Is it the role you want? Create this vision within your Professional Identity.

Engage Your Professional Identity

Only when your Professional Identity is engaged will you honor your true desires and follow the route you created to your final destination. Your Professional Identity will never let you down, confuse you, or act from ego. Your Professional Identity will protect you from lies, detours, and reactive behaviors. Trust it, it will always guide you. Any decisions you make in regards to what jobs to apply for, what interviews to pursue, and what offers to accept or decline should be done from within your Professional Identity.

Once you are clear on how you will show up, what role you will play, and what your Professional Identity is, be faithful to it. These don't change with every interview or new job. You are who you are, and that is the truth. Time and time again, I see job seekers speaking to every job description through their cover letters and morphing into everything the job description wants them to be. This is not only deceitful to the hiring organization, but to yourself. No wonder 50% of American workers are dissatisfied in their roles! Nonprofit professionals are not excluded. They are in the wrong roles!

I highly encourage my clients to remain faithful to their Professional Identity throughout every step of the way. Take pride in it. You have gifts and talents that no one else has. It has taken you courage, discipline, time, and effort to get here. Don't lose sight of that. With clarity around your Professional Identity, interviews are painless, you show up with certainty, and it can be seen and felt. Your new nonprofit employer won't need to spend time trying to figure you out, because you will be transparent and genuine from the beginning.

If you are reading this book and not seeking a new job but are trying to add *more* to your current one, having clarity and being loyal to your Professional Identity will help you gravitate toward creating meaningful work. You will show up differently. You will care more. You will be a happier employee. Your commitment and loyalty will grow and show. This will make the work you produce even more effective and valuable to your organization. You are now operating from a place of strength.

If you are in the market for a new position, after gaining clarity, you will do it with the conviction that this is what your heart truly desires. These are the goals that you will go after. No longer are you at the mercy of the employment market or employer. You've taken control.

Without this clarity, it's pretty easy to confuse *more* with less. You may leap into a position that may resemble what you *think* you want, not what you *know* you want. You will be deceived and make the same mistakes you've made in the past. It can be tempting to say yes to a job just because you receive an offer, not because it is the job that you love and align with.

I attended a conference led by Tony Robbins where he described the six basic human needs that at one time or another we try to fill in life. I believe that these needs also play a role at work. They are:

- Certainty
- Uncertainty
- Significance
- Love/Connection
- Growth
- Contribution

If you were to think back on the different positions you've held in your professional life, can you say which one of the needs above you were trying to meet? In my early years as a recruiter, I played the role of match maker between employer and employee. My Professional Identity was nonexistent, and I was a rookie, pretending that I knew what I was doing. I also tried to act more experienced and to seem unimpressed by my much older and more accomplished interviewees. But I enjoyed the work, and it met a few of my primary needs: significance, uncertainty, and growth.

Human beings crave uncertainty to feel alive and avoid monotony, and in recruiting there is never a dull moment, so that need was certainly met every day. I also was seeking professional growth. I wanted to stretch, grow, and obtain career progression. I wanted to be significant and make a mark for myself.

Once your Professional Identity is redefined, think of the need you'd like to meet in your new role. Is it love and connection, something you might meet by growing your network and becoming good friends with your co-worker? Or is it contribution, where your daily goal might be to contribute at your highest to the mission of the organization and to the well-being of your department? Behind every desire for a role or position, there is always a need trying to be met. Figuring this out while creating your Career Map and developing your Professional Identity will facilitate and strengthen your process.

One of my clients, Marilyn, came to me after having made a few wrong career choices. Her last three positions had led to a resignation, a termination, and, now, a very unhappy current situation. During our clarity session, she came to the conclusion that what had motivated her to pursue and accept all these positions was her need for significance. She admitted to not really aligning with the mission of the organizations, but she did care about the big names of those nonprofits and the significance that their reputations gave her.

Not being clear on what need(s) you are trying to meet in every stage of your professional life makes it difficult to make the right career decisions and moves, and can be confusing. Brutal honesty is also essential here. You have to get clear with yourself so that you can make the right choices.

There is no right or wrong answer when it comes to defining which need you are trying to meet. But if your career goal is blocked by one of your primary needs, then a great place to start is by identifying it.

As you gain clarity, you may also want to define what career success means to you. It might be different than what you think it is! Some feel that career success is getting the job you want, and that once you have been hired, you've succeeded. Others think that success is receiving a promotion every year. For others, it's seeing their paycheck increase over time. There is no right or wrong answer here, either. But once you get clear on what your answer is, you'll also gain, purpose, direction, and intention around it. This will help you move forward and know when you have arrived.

Another element of Career Mapping is deciding whether to create a **two-year or five-year** Career Map. If this is your first time doing it, and most likely it is, I recommend a two-year plan to get you going. Either way, decide your level of participation, choose whether to create a two-year or a five-year plan, and then take action on the steps outlined in each chapter and work on the activities. At the end of the process, you will have a finished and unique Career Map to follow. Don't worry about what happens after you are done creating it. The process is designed to help you make changes along the way. After your Professional Identity is unleashed, it will take over and get you where you want to go.

As you work on gaining clarity, you will also assess your current or former role and job. Notice that "role" and "job" are distinctively different. I believe that the role you play may or may not be aligned with your job. Your job may be to assist a marketing department create innovative copy and educational material. However, your role since day one may have been to track the progress of projects or to keep different departments in the know. It may have been to play gatekeeper or liaison. Your role may have been to delay the process somewhat. Whether unconsciously or consciously, the role you have played may not have served the job. On the other hand, you may have played a leadership role when leadership wasn't expected or required. See how this is an important distinction to make? I want to assure you that these decisions are most often made unconsciously.

Let's work on gaining clarity. Please take some time to answer these questions in your Career Mapping journal:

1. How would you like to describe your professional life two years from now? Be very specific (include your commute, work attire, work hours, what you are eating for lunch, at what time are you eating lunch, compensation, and what your impending promotion or next job look like).

2. In your last role, who did you have to be or become to get and keep your job?

3. In your ideal role, what is the Professional Identity you would like to assume? This should be the very best version of your professional self.

4. What need or needs were you trying to meet in your last role?

5. What need or needs are you trying to meet in your current or future role?

CHAPTER FOUR

Find Your Purpose

"You were put on this earth to achieve your greatest self,
to live out your purpose and to do it courageously."
- Dr. Steve Maraboli

There has to be purpose in all that you do – especially when it comes to your career. Career Mapping adds purpose to your goals. Have you ever asked yourself why you want what you want? Is it coming from deep within, from your own life philosophy, or is it because someone said it was a good idea? Is it because you read an article? Many of my clients and workshop attendees confess not knowing the purpose behind actions or decisions. They get confused with the background noise, other people's opinions, and the "shoulds."

A great way to add purpose to your Career Map and Professional Identity is, again, by being brutally honest with yourself and defining the "why" behind your "what." A question I ask multiple times while doing this process with my clients is: What do you want and why do you want it? Most often, they know the "what" but not the "why." Taking the time to carefully craft your unique Career Map, bringing forth all the exciting goals you want to reach in your professional and personal life and why, will bring energy, drive, and motivation to your journey.

Alexa signed up for private Career Mapping sessions after leaving a job that wasn't making her happy or fulfilled. Her primary goal was to find a new position where she could utilize all her desktop publishing design skills. She felt that she first needed to take a few new classes in desktop publishing to sharpen those skills. After planning out her six- and nine-month goals and seeing that everything was at a standstill until these classes would be completed, I asked her to really think about the reasoning behind her need to take those classes. The classes didn't really offer much of an edge, however she felt it was a deal-breaker if she didn't take them. She felt almost unemployable without them.

It really didn't make much sense. In my experience as a recruiter, I didn't believe that they were all that essential. After much conversation and more reflection, Alexa came to realize that in a previous role she was very impressed by a co-worker who had taken the classes, therefore she felt that she needed them as well to be just as good and as essential in her role. It was never about her interest or her passion, it was about what worked for someone else. Doing what you have concluded you need to do and want to do is very different from doing it because someone else thought it was what you should do, or because someone else did it and it benefited them. When action comes from your unique desires and aspirations, it is so much more powerful. This is what being in the driver's seat looks like.

There is danger in looking outward for what only looking inward can give you. It starts with you. With your interests, your talents, your passion, and your destination. Where would you like to end up? Now add the why. This will give you purpose.

What + why = purpose

As you work on your unique Career Map with the goal of securing a new position or gaining a promotion, take a moment to reflect on what that vision looks like and the why attached to it. If you have been answering the questions in every chapter, you already have a vision for what it is you want. Now take some time to think about why.

The goal in this chapter is to answer as many "whys" as possible. Why do you want that title? Is it because it sounds good, or because it is the natural or expected next step for you? Why are you looking for that level of compensation? Is it because someone said that it is what you should be making, or because that's how much your level of skills and experience command? Getting very clear on the answers to these questions will save you time and frustration as you navigate your Career Map and go from point A to point B.

Let's work on gaining purpose. Please take some time to answer the "why" for your answers to these questions (refer to your answers from Chapter 3):

1. What does your ideal position look like? Why is this important?
2. What are you wearing? Why is this important?
3. What are you eating for lunch? Why is this important?
4. Where is your office located? Why is this important?
5. What is your commute like? Why is this important?
6. What is your work schedule? Why is this important?

7. What is your salary? Why is this important?
8. When will you get your next promotion? Why is this important?
9. Who do you report to? Why is this important?
10. What needs are you trying to meet? Why is this important?

The goal of this exercise is to help you find the meaning in and purpose of your desires and goals. The professionals that have worked intently on their Career Map have found enormous value in this exercise. They have changed some of their "what" answers after realizing that their "why" didn't really align with their Professional Identity. The "why" wasn't really theirs!

What do you value?

Understanding why you do the things that you do gives you the ability to course correct in a more efficient manner. You must first understand where these behaviors are coming from. If you are a person who is chronically late to work, to meetings, and to completing assigned projects and you want to change the habit to a more empowering one, a great place to start would be by asking yourself how this habit is serving you. What is the purpose behind the action? If you have been stuck in your current role and don't know why, think about how this role has served you until now. What has been the purpose behind staying "stuck"? It has served you somehow, how?

Coming to a clear realization of concepts like these might be something new to you, but this is the time to address them and come to terms with them. Something different has to be at play here, and these are the most common areas that need some purging among professionals looking to make their mark and have a successful career in the field of their choosing. Self-analysis and reflection go hand in hand with professional development and growth. I like to remind professionals on this journey not to confuse movement with progress. Being methodical and taking consistent steps forward will get you to where you want to be.

Professionals that successfully navigate their Career Map understand the power of purpose. They use it to their advantage and they add purpose to all that they do. This makes them stand out. Defining your purpose before you start your job search or before you ask for a raise gives you a stronger stance. Knowing your purpose allows you to show up and more easily communicate how you can make a difference within the organization and what makes you unlike others. Many professionals fail to show up at interviews with the ability to speak to what truly makes them a good match for the position or how their purpose aligns with the organization's mission. Not presenting yourself in your true Professional Identity, which should lead with clarity and purpose, is a disservice to you and your interviewer.

Long gone are the days where interviews were an opportunity to fundamentally discuss your skills and experience and assess if there was a personality fit. The 60- or 90-minute meeting used to be just a chance to ask some basic questions about the open position and a time where the interviewer and interviewee would let each other know that there was an interest in continuing the conversation.

The new rule is adding something *more*, and that something *more* comes in the form of a well-thought-out Career Map in hand, clarity, and purpose. Your plan. Your purpose. It also comes with you being in the driver's seat and discerning whether this position truly aligns with your Professional Identity and direction. Whether it aligns with the goals of your future team members and if your contributions will make a difference. Once you have clear career goals, the conversation should have more depth, and at the end of it you should undoubtedly know whether you want to pursue this role or not. My goal is to help you show up at the interview or at work in full consciousness of what you need the outcome to be. Not begging to be hired or given the promotion, but being a key participant in the decision-making and on whether this is a perfect match for you.

For the most part, nonprofit professionals apply for positions at organizations to which they have a personal connection. Whether it's advocating for better healthcare, fighting child trafficking, eliminating hunger, or promoting the arts, there is something for everyone. But sometimes, even when the connection is there, I hear professionals say they feel something is still missing. A connection to the mission does not guarantee a flawless job experience. If that was the case, there would hardly be any turnover in the nonprofit sector.

I strongly believe that it is because there needs to be more than connection to the cause, there must also be purpose. Purpose will turn an average employee into a stellar employee. Purpose brings out the very best in people. Purpose must be individualized. It is that something that will pull you through on the bad days and that will help you assess your next steps. One step forward with purpose gives way to the next step forward with purpose. Purpose breeds purpose. You can't have too much of it. It is the energy behind your journey.

It is important to recognize your purpose and how it aligns with the positions you are pursuing. Go beyond which mission tugs at your heart. Nonprofits are interested in knowing that yes, you do have a passion for their mission, but what is your purpose behind it? It's even more important for you to know it than it is for them to know it. It will help you weed out positions where your purpose will not be in alignment.

How do you know what your purpose is? By discovering your values. What do you value most? In my early career years, I valued growing, learning, and status. My purpose was somewhat vague and maybe frivolous, but I really wanted to be known for being the best and being successful. My purpose was to be the best nonprofit Recruiter I could be, helping nonprofits find the best talent for their open positions.

The purpose of the work that I do now is to help people transform their professional lives through the practice of Career Mapping in a way that gives them clarity, purpose, direction, and intention in the process. Where they make their mark and significant contributions to the nonprofit organizations that they serve. Where they are only accepting jobs that they truly love!

When you operate with a purposeful Professional Identity, everything makes sense and every action is deliberate. You want to make a difference, and you do. You find yourself contributing at a level that was not there before, and there is so much more meaning to your actions. Suddenly, the tasks that were mundane are now vital. Is it a beautiful thing when career and purpose come together.

Here is another exercise to help you gain purpose. Please take some time to answer these questions in your Career Mapping journal:

1. What is the purpose of your current Professional Identity?
2. List three ways to add purpose to your current role.
3. What purpose would you like to have in your next role?

CHAPTER FIVE

Set Your Direction

With clarity and purpose in hand, you set out to create your direction. This should be a lot of fun, as it allows you to be inventive, dream big, and stretch your imagination.

By now, you have decided whether you want to create a two-year or five-year Career Map. This is strictly your preference, but if you're brand new to this process, I recommend you start with a two-year map until you sort out the basic elements and get a good handle on the flow of things. A year into it, you will most likely have a clear vision of your five- year plan, a plan unique to you and what you love.

Now that you know where you want to end up, let's set some goals to get you there. Where do you see yourself in two years? When I met with my career counselor, she tasked me with creating a vision of my Professional Identity, my purpose, and my end destination. After doing that, I took time to take a hard look at the three elements of my Career Map and answer these very important questions:

- Where I have been?
- Where am I now?
- Where am I going?

This assessment told me a story. Just like your assessment will tell you a story. It will also outline the steps you need to take to get to your goals.

For many people, it proves to be very challenging to get from point A to point B. They get frustrated and make many, many U-Turns, wasting lots of valuable time and gas in the form of energy! This is because they have skipped steps.

When I work with professionals who are creating their first Career Map, having clarity and purpose brings out a very clear direction. The course then maps out almost to perfection. The map is inspiring, it's motivating, and most, importantly, it is theirs. Their GPS is tuned in and ready to take them to where they want to go. Every step builds on the next.

With a Career Map you can't take shortcuts, because your shortcut is your map. Professionals with a map achieve their goals much faster, and with more joy, enthusiasm, excitement, and calculated risks!

With your inventory in hand, a vivid picture of what role you want to play, and a handle on what your unique gifts are, you can now list the gaps between your now and your next.

In Chapter Two, you took a professional inventory. Please revisit and determine what skills and experiences you need to strengthen to get you to the next level. Be honest with yourself. If you are low in the "interpersonal skills" category, don't rate yourself high. If your management skills need improvement, reflect that on your assessment. This is for you and only you to use. It doesn't serve you to glorify or make up skills while taking inventory. This exercise will help you identify the soft and hard skills you need to strengthen in order to get to the job of your dreams.

Closing the gaps

Let's start with those skills and experiences that you need to build up for your ideal job. The next step will be to list ways in which you will address those weaknesses and attach SMART goals to these steps. In Chapter 1, I described SMART goals.

SMART goals are:

- **Specific:** Not vague. Exactly what do you want?
- **Measurable:** Goals should be quantified. How will you know if you've achieved it or not?
- **Attainable:** Being honest with yourself about what you can reasonably accomplish at this point in your career, while taking into consideration your current responsibilities.
- **Realistic:** It's got to be doable, real and practical.
- **Time-based:** Associate a time frame with each goal. When should you complete the goal?

For example, let's say you've discovered that your purpose in life is doing all that you can to make sure that no one goes to sleep hungry in the city of Dallas. One of your goals may be to secure a position at a nonprofit whose mission is to help eradicate hunger because this aligns with your purpose. You have a background in marketing and greatly like this work. Within a Marketing Manager position, your Professional Identity wants to play the role of change agent and innovator. In doing this exercise, you realize that you lack social media and website management skills and experience – two skills often required in marketing positions. Your SMART goals may be to take some classes, read some books, get a certificate in website management, or ask a friend to teach you how to do these things.

Let's break it down further with one of the two skills listed as a weakness:

- **Specific:** Take an online website management class.
- **Measurable:** When I meet this goal, can I manage a website? Yes or no?
- **Attainable:** I have multiple ways to accomplish this within my limits.
- **Realistic:** I have the time, means, ability, and access to learn this skill.
- **Time-based:** I will be proficient at website management in three months.

If you methodically do this practice with all of the gaps that appear on your Career Map and work diligently on them, you will no doubt get to your dream job. You will arrive with confidence and displaying the talents you were meant to own. Be cautious of distractions and of making things more complicated than they should be. Don't lose the clarity that you have gained, and do create all your SMART goals in your Professional Identity. It will never fail you. Do something daily that moves the needle in all of your goals. Even if that is just making a call, sending an email, or doing research. Take an action that adds progress, not just movement.

Many of my clients were able to work on their gaps while holding full-time positions. You don't have to be unemployed to work on a Career Map. You can transform your career and find your *more* while working. You can create your Career Map and benefit from being employed to get you there. Going through this process first and then involving others at work has been proven to be beneficial and may be something to seriously consider. You always want to operate from a place of being transparent and benefiting from collaboration with your work team.

A perfect time to address an interest in something *more* at work is during your performance review. If the review is too far in the future, you can request a meeting with your supervisor sooner. This candid conversation with your supervisor about wanting to learn website management, and exploring if this is something that your organization can facilitate either through a paid class or in house training, is something that should be regarded as a great sign by your supervisor. It's a sign of commitment to professional development, to gaining new skills that will benefit the organization, and to contributing at a higher level. All win-win!

Another common scenario is being in a position where your GPS hits a dead end. Sometimes, professionals who thought they were in dead end positions have had a complete change of mind after gaining clarity and purpose. In their true Professional Identity, they were able to identify opportunities that they had missed when they were out of focus. Your best role could be your current role. Before quitting too soon, assess your current situation and compare it with your dream job. Could you make your mark here? If you were to show up tomorrow in your Professional Identity and play a role that would serve you and the organization at the highest level, could you be happy and find your more here? Be methodical and take time to see where you want to go and where you are now. It could be that by closing the gaps, you can turn your existent position into your ideal position!

How do you identify future goals?

What do you fantasize about when you think of your dream job? Your future goals are listed in your dream job description. Take a moment to see what things in your dream job description you wish for and what things you already have. Those things that are missing are your future goals. Run them through the

SMART goal test and go after them. Remember: "Goals are the stepping stone of success."

Where you want to be -
where you are now = SMART goals

Many Career Mappers worry about not having the right goals in place or about knowing what goals to reach for. The gap between where you are now and where you want to go *is* a goal. This gap should be closed by creating SMART goals around them. This is the simplest and most accurate method of identifying your career goals and getting to work on them! Be focused, confident, and committed.

As part of the goal-setting process, it helps to identify the difference between short-term goals and long-term goals. For example, developing the habit of finishing your projects ahead of deadline is a short-term goal; getting an MBA is a long-term goal. Easy, right?

How about getting a promotion? Short- or long-term goal? It depends. In most professionals' minds, it should be a short-term goal. But it usually takes longer than expected. Having your unique Career Map will help you hugely in being visible within your organization and beyond. Why? Because you will show up confident, happy, centered, and with clarity on where you are and where you want to be. You will strategize with leadership about your next career moves and your potential in the organization. You and your supervisors will both have a clear vision of your aspirations, motivation, skills, and experience. It will be so much easier for them to manage your expectations and you, theirs. You will also be certain about who you are. A professional with a Career Map is unstoppable. Sometimes we overestimate what we can do in a year and underestimate what we can accomplish in five. Time goes by quickly; don't be a victim to it. Maximize every second and make each one count!

How Career Mapping helps with career advancement

Many wonder why getting a promotion can be a struggle, and if you look closely at the reason, it's obvious that it's not lack of effort or interest on either side. It's a lack of a GPS on both sides. By the time this book is published, I'll be working on another book where I teach organizations how to have Career Mapping conversations with all the members of their staff. Discussions around career advancement are usually mysterious and tense. Both parties involved may have different expectations. Some employers don't have a clear vision or direction of departmental growth, or may not know how committed an employee is. Some employees may not be aware of the employer's expansion plans or outlined career trajectories for their staff. This is just a short list of many other possibilities that make this process hard to manage for the employer and employee. While things are still changing for the better in this arena, take control of your professional destiny and approach this subject with management in a positive and empowering manner. It may sound scary, because it's not a common practice, but it is a great start. With a complete Career Map, this discussion can be seamless and powerful.

Set your direction, know where you are, change course, keep moving, and don't stop. There is so much joy to be found in setting your GPS on the road to success. Your success. Your way. If you learn anything while reading this book, it should be the belief that you can transform your professional career and get out of a career rut or career limbo with the right map. Don't use other people's maps, they may not be going to where you want to go. Imagine trying to get from Chicago to NYC, but your map's route is toward San Francisco! You will never get where you want to go!

One of my clients, who we will call Melanie, always knew that her calling was to help others.

At the same time, she didn't know in what capacity and how she would do it. After going through the Career Mapping process and being inspired by the realization that she could create a successful map for herself, she almost instantly and effortlessly designed a five-year Career Map. She loved where she currently worked, and so she incorporated her current position into the map. She wanted to stay and grow with the organization. Her Career Map confirmed that she was happy with the duties in her position and the role that she played. Before Career Mapping, she knew that she wanted to help people. But after Career Mapping, she had a clear direction of how to do it – and now has even more goals that she would like to pursue in the near future. She was extremely inspired by the potential in herself and within her current role. She gained new enthusiasm and drive, and saw new opportunities and possibilities where she wasn't seeing them before. Melanie is well on her way to reaching her goals and going on to the next ones.

For setting goals, I like to recommend revisiting the map every six months, which mitigates the potential for getting lost or sidetracked on the journey. It also provides an opportunity to assess the accuracy of your skills assessment and measure your progress in skill development. In essence, it provides you an opportunity to discover whether you are on the right road before too much time has passed.

Important questions to ask when you revisit your Career Map include:

- Am I still passionate?
- Am I continuing to develop new skills?
- Am I getting closer to my goals?

If the answer to any of these questions is "no," then you have encountered an *aha* flag. Notice that I did not use the term *red* flag. This is intentional. A *red* flag has negative connotations. *Aha* flags are actually good things. They serve as a part of your internal GPS system to help you progress according to your career map. An *aha* flag is a repositioning notification that lets you know that either you are off track or your map needs tweaking.

Aha flags, if we pay attention, can guide us in the right direction. As we work our maps, we should remain mindful of feelings of dissatisfaction, boredom, or lack of enthusiasm – these are all *aha* flags signaling that something is off. *Aha* flags can happen at any time, not just during your bi-annual Career Map review. A Career Map is not a passive exercise. Instead, it is a progressive evaluation that ultimately leads to career satisfaction and success.

As you pay attention to the *aha* flags that can arise along your journey, it is important to emphasize that your journey is just that – yours. No one can tell you which road is the right one for you but *you*. Even when your path seems right to everyone else, if it doesn't fill you with passion and excitement, then you may be heading in the wrong direction.

This is the power of a Career Map. It gives you clarity by telling you what it is that you want, then it tells you why you want it and draws the steps for getting there. Imagine having the use of this tool from your very first job! But don't dwell on that thought! It is never too late to use the power of a Career Map, even if you are well into your career journey.

Let's work on setting your direction. Please take some time to answer these questions in your Career Mapping journal:

1. List five short-term goals (six months – one year) and run them through the SMART test.
2. List five long-term goals (one – two years) and run them through the SMART test.

CHAPTER SIX

Gain Intention

You've gained clarity, purpose, and direction. Now it's time to set your intention. What is intention when it comes to your Career Map? Allow me to illustrate it with one of my clients' experiences. Anthony engaged in Career Mapping when he was actively pursuing a promotion as a program manager, a completely different role from what he had been doing. When we first started working together, he appeared to be certain of what he wanted to do, why he wanted to do it, and where he wanted to be, but he lacked focus on how he was going to accomplish the end goal. Time and time again, when he encountered an obstacle or things didn't go his way, he became frustrated. His lack of intention was clearly visible. When I asked about his intention as it related to his career goals, he was at a loss.

Intention is the last piece of the puzzle that glues everything together to help you reach your professional goals. In Career Mapping, purpose is inward and gives you meaning; intention is outward and is something you give of yourself to others. You give intention to your role, your organization, your team, and the world. Anthony's quest for a promotion had drive, but he missed adding intention to the puzzle. He needed this last piece to make the leap and secure the role he desired as quickly and efficiently as possible.

By this stage you have your what, why, and where. Now let's dive into the how. How will you do all of this? What is the intention? In the course of action(s) that you have come up with, how you direct all the steps and get to your destination is just as important as where you end up.

Nonprofits are always trying to find the ideal professional. The person who is going to dedicate all their talents, skills, and efforts to pursuing the organization's principal mission. Ideally this person is as interested in aligning their Professional Identity as the organization is in aligning their mission. This professional, in an ideal world, has the intention to grow, contribute, and succeed.

How you show up is integral to your success and contribution. In Chapter 3, we discussed the creation of your Professional Identity and how you were going to show up. Let's go deeper with this concept. Part of your Professional Identity is recognizing your intention for pursuing your goals. What is your intent in charting the course that you have identified? Aside from being gainfully employed, what major contributions will you make in order to make your mark? As you are committing to living your professional life on your terms, your intentions will help align with others along your path, as well as the projects and the outcomes that you are interested in pursuing.

When I founded CNP, my primary intention was to create a company different from any other that I had worked for. I wanted to provide formidable staffing services to the nonprofit sector, and I wanted to offer those services to nonprofits across the country. My intention was and still is to offer the best staffing experience to employers and job seekers. I also wanted to become an employer of choice for recruiters and create a company that was fertile ground for professionals seeking to make a difference in the nonprofit sector. I wanted to lead a team that was knowledgeable, happy, and fulfilled. I wanted to help them make their professional and personal dreams come true. These intentions dictated and/or enhanced my what, my where, and my why.

My intentions lead all my actions. How I hired, how I grew the company, what organizations I pursued to work with, and what my five-year business plan looked like. Fast forward ten years, and I still have some of the same intentions, plus I have added the intention of being a servant leader – innovative, and changing lives through the work that I do. How I would do it is with integrity, passion, drive, and big vision.

Please answer these questions in your Career Mapping journal:

1. What is your primary professional focus?
2. What question do you ask yourself most often based on this focus?

My primary professional focus is improving results and performance. Seeing how professionals make a 180-degree shift in their professional lives, after Career Mapping, gives me tremendous satisfaction. I enjoy pushing through tough challenges and helping others pushing through their challenges, limitations, and fears.

The question I most often ask myself is, "How do I make this better?" My intention for most of what I do is to make it better. To do better each time, to raise the standards, and to stretch the limits.

If you think about these two questions and answer with brutal honesty, you will find your real intentions behind the SMART goals you've set out to meet.

To be intentional at every step is to go toward your professional dream without being ambivalent. It's going at it with certainty and knowing. Whether you recognize them or not, you have intentions for most, if not all, of the areas of your life.

Intention gives your professional life animation and power. Yes! If purpose is the gas in your car, then intention is your set of wheels. This is how you do it: Let the world see and hear your intentions at every step of the way. And be clear, very clear, about what they are. They are a key piece of your compass. Going about transforming your professional life for the better without intention is like going for a drive without wheels. You won't be able to go very far.

If, after answering the questions listed above, you are not quite happy with the intention(s) you carry, whether because they are weak, ill-intentioned (it happens), or they don't serve you in a positive way, a very effective way to make bring them into alignment with your Professional Identity is to change your focus and ask yourself a better question.

While creating Anthony's Career Map and working on his intention, he identified that his primary professional focus was: How do I get the best from this position? This focus kept him constantly looking for ways in which his organization, supervisor, and team members served *him* and what they had to offer *him*. His primary professional focus or question did not serve him well. He maintained a state of unease and was guarded. At any sign of someone else getting *more* than him in any sense, he became frustrated and unhappy. After grueling work and reflection, he decided to change the primary focus of his Professional Identity to: How do I offer *my* best to this position and my team members, supervisor, and organization?

This simple change in grammar and thinking changed his world. Once he made this intention part of his Professional Identity, many doors opened for him. His new intention was an outward goal, something outside of himself and for the benefit of others. This change made his clarity, purpose, and direction even more substantial. He felt more at ease. He was able to let his guard down and show up as a person who was genuine, trustworthy, and confident.

When we have not proactively taken the time to think about why we do the things we do and we operate mindlessly, it can be difficult to let go of some things and make positive changes. Ego gets in the way, and a weak intention becomes your false identity and takes over your true destiny. But with some reflection and a plan, it loosens its grip and sets you free.

The power of intention will make your map ten times sharper and will get you through even when you encounter bad weather. Trust it, it will not fail you! Remember to ask yourself the right questions. Bad intentions come from the wrong focus and the wrong questions. Meditate on these concepts and keep digging until the truth surfaces. You will recognize the truth once you see it. It will feel comfortable and it will fit like a glove. You will regain control of your career destiny with renewed enthusiasm and drive.

While working on her first Career Map, Evelyn enthusiastically set out to map out and visualize the steps to get to where she wanted to go in her professional trajectory. She had been meeting positive professional milestones at a comfortable pace. With Career Map in hand, she realized that by being intentional, she could make the best use of her time and make smarter decisions when it came to seeking promotions and more responsibilities. Setting intentional goals that aligned with her Professional Identity helped her stay focused on what she was working toward, but also allowed her to check in with herself when she was avoiding any of the SMART goals she set for herself. Evelyn found that coming back to her intentions and motivations was critical as she self-assessed and re-routed her Career Map when necessary. She felt that as a result of being intentional with her Career Map, she found more direction and purpose within her career aspirations. She frequently asked herself the hard questions to ensure that she was heading in the right direction. She was happy to have found that by being intentional, both her direction and purpose became clearer, too. Her best outcome from this process was how things fell into place for her with ease and enjoyment. And very little re-routing!

As you embark on your Career Mapping journey, you may discover some emotions and limiting beliefs that might hold you back from being as intentional as you can be – or that may create the wrong intentions on your path. Empowering emotions and disempowering emotions affect us on a daily basis. There is a lot of emotion tied to your professional success and your Professional Identity. When creating a Career Map, you want to focus on emotions that empower you and that facilitate your best expression. You have a choice. You can choose to feel ignored by your manager, unappreciated, or disliked. Or you can choose to feel excited, passionate, optimistic, and valued. It really depends on what you choose to focus on. It is highly effective to find and use the right emotions to get you there. You might have the best-created map in the world, but without the right set of emotions and intentions, the route will be bumpy.

Choose wisely. Training yourself to feel good on a day-to-day basis will give you a great advantage in every sense. You will make wiser decisions when you choose to be in an empowered state, and you will gain both self-confidence as well as the confidence of your team members and supervisors. Your work results will be of higher caliber and you will be more satisfied of your accomplishments.

Oftentimes the disempowering and empowering emotions we carry around our work are born out of bad or great work-related experiences. Take some time to think of your current position or past positions and your personal experiences in them. How have they affected the way you view your work life today? In helping you stir up some buried memories, let's became brutally honest as we reflect.

Please take some time to answer these questions in your Career Mapping journal:

1. What are your three worst work experiences?
2. What are your three best work experiences?
3. What are your five most enjoyable work tasks?
4. What are your five most avoided work tasks?

Notice how taking the time to dig deep and write your thoughts clears a lot of your thinking. Maybe it's confusing at first, which is normal, but if you stay with it, you realize that a lot of your disempowering emotions come from bad experiences and are often unresolved issues you carry with you. As you may notice from answering the questions above, you also have had positive experiences, even if you have not chosen to focus on them. Why is that? Quite simply, it's because as humans we try to avoid pain; we are conditioned to survive, and so by replaying the bad scenarios in your mind, you might think that you will avoid them. In fact, you attract them even more.

As part of your Career Mapping process, you want to let go of anything that holds you down and doesn't serve you. You will find that you will make choices at every turn of your Career Map. These are *your* choices, not your spouse's, co-workers' or managers'. Yours and only yours. These choices will always be accompanied by your intentions. Don't let anyone influence your decision-making. Once you have done the hard work of reflecting and peeling the layers to uncover who you truly are and to unveil your true Professional Identity, the rest comes easy. Your Professional Identity will be guided by your intentions and your intentions will facilitate decision-making. There will be many. Will you be true to your Career Map?

Please answer these questions in your Career Mapping journal:

1. What career choices have you made in the past that have yielded successful outcomes?
2. What career choices have you made in the past that have yielded negative outcomes?
3. If you could do it over with what you know now, what would you do differently?
4. What five new choices could you make that would improve the quality of your professional life today?

Once you change the quality of your emotions, you will make better choices. A change in your emotions can transform your professional behavior, which will in turn impact your actions. The right emotions, carried over into your Career Map, can take you straight to your desire outcome. Emotions like confidence, courage, and determination can add that extra mileage to your Career Map! Focus on better emotions, and let them create your intentions to success. The intention you set forward will make your journey speedy, productive, and successful. You will make your mark!

CHAPTER SEVEN

Yellow, Green, and Red Lights

After going through all the steps and re-gaining power over your professional life, you might find bliss and fulfillment – or more confusion and uncertainty. Don't despair. This is all part of the process, and it's temporary. You might second-guess your clarity, purpose, direction or intention. I want you to know that this is all normal. The gratification and outcomes will far outweigh any discomfort that you may find along the way. When I decided to transform my career and go for the vision that I had, there were countless times when I thought my steps were futile. I second-guessed myself over and over again. My career counselor warned me of the possibility of encountering yellow and red street lights in my journey, and encouraged me to charge through the process in spite of them.

What things might go wrong in this journey? I will try to manage some of your expectations and share with you the most common scenarios that I have seen my clients go through. One of the first things that appeared for Anthony while in the process was **doubting** whether he even needed a Career Map. His first instinct was yes, but when faced with the process and the work involved it all seem pretty simple. He felt as if he had touched, at some point in his life, on all four aspects, so why go at it in such a methodical way? Couldn't he just wing it and continue doing what he had been doing until now?

In spite of his doubts, he engaged in the Career Mapping process because he didn't have "much to lose," he said. He also trusted his friend that introduced him to Career Mapping and who had seen remarkable results. Thankfully, and for the sake of his bright future, he stuck with it, and shortly after starting the process he realized that winging it would not have been an option. Winging it had brought him to where he was now, which was nowhere close to where he wanted to be.

Although these steps might seem ordinarily simple, when it comes to Career Mapping and many other things in life, it's not what you know, but what you do. I'll say it again: It's not what you know, but what you do that will make a difference. The way to overcome doubt is to trust. Fake trust if you must until you get comfortable, but trust that your Professional Identity will get you where you want to be. Stick with the process; work on the steps. One by one, these steps will build upon each other. If it was easy and unnecessary, there would hardly be anyone feeling stuck at work or in career limbo. When in doubt, forge forward!

Going through your professional life lacking fullness of experience, joy, and self-expression because of self doubt, is like going through life missing a few of your senses. You have the right to make smart choices, chart a path, make your mark, take the driver's seat, and create your legacy. Your unique contributions to the world!

One other emotion that often shows up is **fear**, fear of not being in control and of making the wrong moves. If up until now you have let other people chart your career path, it might be a little frightening to take that control back. Many of my clients have allowed this for far too long. They have just not paid that much attention, or have decided to take the path of least resistance, which seems on the surface to be the easier thing to do. Relying on sources outside of yourself like your spouse, employer, family and friends might lead you to the wrong destination. You might have had to relinquish control because you were uncertain about your career moves, or unsure about the best decisions to make. Once in the Career Mapping process, reclaiming the driver's seat might make you fearful. You might be afraid of asking those who have been in control to step down and let you make your own decisions guided by your Career Map and Professional Identity and not by what they think is best for you.

You might fear your own decision-making once you are in the driver's seat. Are you making the right turns? Are you going in the right direction? This is all very, very normal, and it is your mind trying to protect you. In the middle of my Career Mapping process, I wondered if I ever would see all the SMART goals I was setting come to materialize. My goals were very ambitious. Who was I to make them happen? I certainly didn't have a long track record of achievement. All I had was the desire to do something different and maximize my potential. Many nights I laid awake, wondering if I should quiet the voices in my head and play it safe. I wondered if I would be better off staying in my comfort zone, but the more time, thought, and effort I put into my Career Mapping, the more I knew that playing it safe was not what my soul desired and what my Professional

Identity was about. Career Mapping gave me the courage necessary to make the changes I craved.

Melanie had some fears surface as well when she was working on her Career Map. She was fearful of going for "too much" and, in the end, not living up to her potential. She feared not gaining the support of those around her and making it difficult to fit in at the workplace. Ultimately her desires to make a real difference and to grow trumped these fears. She was committed to materializing her dream of becoming so much more for the company she worked for and for herself. Melanie maintained her focus on her long-term and short-term SMART goals, and recently reported being extremely content with her accomplishments and determination. She confessed that if she had stopped in the face of fear, she would still be dancing around the idea of being fully happy at work and that she would have probably left her position thinking that it was an external problem and not an internal one.

Another obstacle that might hinder the success of your Career Mapping process is feeling as if it is too late to take on this journey, too late to divert the course. It is never too late! I've worked with professionals at every stage of their careers, and they have been able to arrive at their dream destination with the help of a Career Map. Consider the alternative: spending two, five, or ten more years in a position that is either not fulfilling, or is not helping you create your dream job. Imagine discovering you have been wasting your time and undermining your potential! Think about how lost you would feel if you discover you've been traveling, but have been walking down the wrong road. It is far better to undergo challenging reflection and preparation now than to regret not doing so later. The yearning for *more* will always be there if you don't stop to figure out what it is and how to fulfill it.

In addition to fear and doubt, you might encounter a bit of resistance. **Resistance** from yourself and others who might think they know what is best for you better than you do. If you have relied heavily on the help of others to determine what decisions you need to make in your professional life, once you stop relying less on others and allowing your Professional Identity and Career Map to be your guiding force, others might resist this. How could you not want or need their opinion anymore? They've helped you until now; you wouldn't be where you are without them. Understanding their motives isn't really that important. What matters is that what you have been doing until now has not worked – and this is exactly why you should be firm in your decision to follow your own instincts.

Doing this work requires that you shut down outside voices during the process, so that your conclusions and decisions are yours. They should reflect your clarity, purpose, and intention.

They should direct you to your unique destination. This realization is not only difficult for you, but also for those that have been in the driver's seat in your place. Your boss might offer resistance to your new enthusiasm and intention. Even as they appreciate the new and improved you, they might fear that you may leave soon or in the near future. Here is where having a frank conversation about your career goals will be very helpful. You want to make them part of the plan, whether that is by working with you on meeting your career goals at your current organization, or creating a transition. Don't let the fear of this conversation hold you back. You might be surprised by the positive outcomes.

You might offer resistance to yourself consciously or unconsciously as you chart unknown territory. This is also normal, and being aware of it out of the gate makes it easier to manage. Resistance might come in the form of you not committing to and meeting your SMART goals. Time might pass by and you miss your deadlines, lose focus, or suddenly get very busy at work and not have the time to work on your long- and short-term goals.

This will happen, and it is okay. When you find yourself off-road, gently steer yourself back onto it. There is no need to despair or beat yourself up. Everyone in the quest to achieving their professional dreams encounter detours, dead ends, and traffic jams. Keep your eyes on the prize, and let your Professional Identity lead the way. Dust off your two-year Career Map and get back on track. Don't give up because you find a few bumps in the road. They will always be there.

Your analytical thinking might also get in the way. You might confuse acting from a position of strength with acting from a position of weakness. Inner strength and conviction of what your intentions are will come in handy during this process. Ask yourself, when you are at a standstill, if you are stopping because you strongly feel that you need to, or because you strongly think that you can't continue. There are many decisions that you will have to make on this journey. At every turn, you will have to decide what the next step is. This can be overwhelming if you get sidetracked and don't consult with your Career Map frequently. Check in with yourself and make sure that your decisions come from your strengths and not your weaknesses.

In my personal Career Mapping journey, I had many decisions to make. Did I want to stay in my comfort zone, or did I want to take a leap of faith? Taking a leap of faith is what I decided to do out of strength. Out of knowing that I had the will, emotions, Professional Identity, vision, skills, and experience necessary to make the leap. Did I have it all? Of course not, but I chose to focus on what I did have. And I was convinced that I would add what was missing along the way.

Should I have chosen to stay in my comfort zone, this would have clearly been a decision made out of weakness. Weakness of not believing in myself, of not trusting, of having a weak vision in my purpose and intention. I worked on each Career Mapping step as I advanced towards my goals.

Losing sight of the end goal as well as focusing on the wrong emotions will slow your progress. You will hit roadblocks – that's no secret, and it should not come as a surprise if you got as far as reading this chapter. Practicing being in an empowered state on a daily basis will help you manage your emotions and operate from a place of ease. Being gentle and patient with yourself during this process will keep you on course.

Sure, this process can be challenging and a little scary. Why wouldn't it be? It is life-transforming, and growth pains are par for the course. But don't despair. When you find yourself wandering away from your Career Map, go back and read the answers to your clarity questions. Give yourself smaller, daily goals to meet. These goals will add up to your bigger ones.

Your mind will try to protect you and distract you to keep you safe. Distractions play a big role in your journey. Choose wisely: You can choose to go on the scenic route and make this journey as beautiful as it can be. Career Mapping facilitates that. Or you can kick and scream your whole way through. The beauty of this is that with a Career Map in hand, your GPS will limit the traffic jams, detours, and dead ends, making your journey as enjoyable and scenic as possible. Isn't that amazing? And worth the trip?

Remind yourself that you are not going to achieve your dreams in the safety of your comfort zone. Your mind will try to make things complicated. Don't let it. You might overthink things and try to take back roads not drawn on your map. This may lead to major delays, making it harder to get back on the expressway to your dream destination. Don't do that; stay true to the original plan. The rockier it gets, the more you need to stay focused until you get on the fast lane again!

One mental hack that always helps and empowers me and my clients is thinking of the person they have to become to meet their goals, to envision how they will be different once they arrive at their destination. And why it matters.

Please take some time to answer these questions in your Career Mapping journal:

1. Who do you have to become to meet your Career Mapping goals?
2. Once you've met your short-term and long-term SMART goals, how will you be different from who you are now?
3. Why does it matter to become this person?

Stay on the course, trust yourself, and trust your map. You've come a long way on the road to success. Enjoy every minute of it!

Conclusion

Every Career Mapping journey is unique. It's supposed to be. Many come to it after years of wandering and being lost. Some come to it out of curiosity; others were invited to the journey; and some are still just on the sidelines watching others who have a unique Career Map and are succeeding at making their mark. They are watching from a distance as professionals who are being of service live a life of fulfillment, contribution, and ease. Career Mapping is for everyone. Embarking on a journey that guarantees moving you along and arriving at a destination of your choice is your professional right and duty. Career Mapping helps you show up confidently. Ready to make your mark.

Career Mapping will be one of your biggest rewards and source of joy. Stick with the process. The more difficult it seems or the more resistance that shows up, the more you need it. Keep this in mind and let it be a confirmation that you are on the right path. Look forward to making every day a Friday, making your mark, and being the creator of your destiny. Taking back control and getting back on course will make a significant impact on the quality of your professional and personal life. It will also inspire others and shift your ability (and theirs) to contribute at a higher level. The impact a happy professional makes to the nonprofit sector and to the world is priceless.

One of the many joys of my journey has been to bring others with me. By getting out of my comfort zone and charting the way for myself and my peers. Leading by example and showing them the possibilities that are to be found on the other side of the journey. Bringing others with you enhances the journey. Give it a try.

Remember the process. Work on the five steps in the order listed with consistency and determination, and you will get there – with minimal struggle and re-routes:

Step 1: Achieve Clarity
Step 2: Find Purpose
Step 3: Set Direction

Step 4: Gain Intention
Step 5: Prepare for Obstacles

Once you understand where you are and you figure out your destination, then you must assess the gap, i.e., what missing skills, if any, could keep you from achieving your goal. Once you identify those missing skills, then it's time to get to work and set yourself to developing those skills. This may mean taking on new responsibilities in your current position, seeking out a different professional opportunity, or volunteering in a role that helps you develop the skills or experience that you need to reach your destination.

Enjoy the process. Get in the driver's seat and tell yourself that you decide whether it will be the scenic route or the bumpy one. Get on the expressway to fulfilling your career dreams. It has happened for countless others. Behind every happy and successful nonprofit professional, there is a Career Map.

Don't be afraid to be creative and original. It's okay if your goal is something that has never been accomplished. Be open to your creativity. Let your light shine bright. It doesn't serve to play it small. Take risks, make smart moves, and be loyal to your Career Map once you create it. It will take you to amazing places.

My wish for you is that you reveal your Professional Identity and, as you create your unique Career Map, that you set out on a journey of reflection, discovery, and creation. Bring to light the professional life you were meant to live. Visualize it and manifest it. In spite of fears, regrets, bumps on the road, and detours. Commit to materializing your dreams. Create bold goals and go for them.

A nonprofit professional who is determined, focused, joyful, and fearless is a game changer. Dedicating your talents to making a difference in the nonprofit sector already means that you are committed to changing the world. Do it with enthusiasm and with your genuine Professional Identity leading the way.

No regrets. With eyes wide open and a Career Map, you are on your way to creating the life that you want. One step at a time. Reaching one goal after the other at a consistent pace. Take charge. You don't want to wake up and realize that you have been on the wrong course or someone else's course your entire professional life. You already know what *not* having a Career Map feels like. Try something different. Commit to giving yourself a chance to make your mark, your way.

The nonprofit sector is dependent on professionals who are dedicated to raising the standards and who are committed to collectively improving the lives of many. This movement can only be successfully accomplished by improving your own life first. Don't hold back. Raise the standards for yourself; show up ready to make your mark. Be brave and know that the world counts on each of us to continue creating a realm of possibility for all of humanity.

If you have chosen your destination carefully and with honesty, then following your Career Map will bring you professional fulfillment and the kind of success that does not come from the acquisition of a title, or the attainment of a position. If you work your map and revisit it often, you will discover that it is in the pursuit of happiness that there is joy, and that is true success. Decide that from now on, work means contribution. Check in with yourself often and see if you are constantly growing and contributing. This is truly where the spice of life is: growth and contribution. Career Map your way to making your mark!

Acknowledgements

To God for opening my heart and pouring love, understanding, and compassion. For leading the way and giving me the courage to start and finish this book. Before I typed one word in any of the chapters, I prayed that he would align my thoughts and message to His will. I wanted Him to use me as an instrument to change the lives of many like he changed mine.

This movement was visualized by my always thoughtful, giving, and keen husband, Doug. He said I didn't have a choice but to share my gifts. He said it wasn't up to me, that this is what I needed to do, and that the world was waiting for my message. That I could only hide for so long. That this was my path. Thank you, Doug. You believed in me when I didn't. You saw the bigger picture when I hid behind my short vision. You seduced my inner author, set her free, and gave her a voice.

In 2015, Doug started describing to me the difference I could make with my message, but I waited, I delayed, I stayed in my comfort zone even when I knew that I wanted to share it with the world. I talked about a book, I talked about more workshops but really didn't do much about it. Until the desire of bringing this movement to life became an obsession and I couldn't stop thinking about it.

I'm thankful to my children Andrew and Allena, who ate on paper plates for a month because I needed to save time in every area of my life to finish this book. To my team members at work who cheered me on and created space for this project. I'm grateful for their protection of my time and for taking care of everything so that I could write. I couldn't do any of this without your help, encouragement, love, and support.

To my friends who answered all my job-related questions time and time again and thought that I was the bravest person for taking on this journey. You know who you are, and you are always in my heart.

To the Morgan James Publishing team: Special thanks to David Hancock, CEO & Founder for believing in me and my message. To my Author Relations Manager, Gayle West, thanks for making the process seamless and easy. Many more thanks to everyone else, but especially Jim Howard, Bethany Marshall, and Nickcole Watkins.

Finally, a special thanks to all those nonprofit professionals that allowed me to witness how they created and set into practice a beautiful and unique Career Map that took them exactly where they wanted to be. Thanks for allowing yourselves to be vulnerable, to share, and to trust.

About the Author

Nurys Harrigan-Pedersen is a talent management and staffing expert with 20 years' experience connecting employers with talent and professionals with careers in the nonprofit sector. A native of The Dominican Republic, she began her career in executive search and recruiting in New York City. In 2006, she founded Careers In Nonprofits (CNP), now among the leading nonprofit staffing firms in the US. Careers

In Nonprofits serves both the employer and jobseeker market in Atlanta, Chicago, Washington, D.C., and San Francisco, focusing on a range of careers from entry-level to executive positions in temporary and permanent capacities and in the ever-expanding temp-to-permanent market.

Nurys' insider perspective on the workplace expands to the private sector. She is frequently invited to conduct Career Mapping workshops by employers and industry associations, and shares career-building and job search advice through her online column *Career Q&A with Nurys*.

In summer 2012, Nurys launched the "I Love My Job" campaign to encourage jobseekers to "really go after what they want to do" and accept only those jobs that are in line with their career goals.

Nurys has a Master's degree in labor relations and human resources management from Baruch College - City University of New York, and a bachelor's degree in public administration. Nurys is active in the Association of Fundraising Professionals (AFP), the Society for Human Resource Management (SHRM), the American Society of Association Executives (ASAE), and the Association Forum of Chicagoland.

She lives with her husband and two young children in Northern Virginia.

Thank You

Thank you for reading! As a special gift for my readers, I've offering a 30 minute discovery session to help you figure out exactly where you are on your career path and give you a foundation for figuring out what to do next to create, find, or turn your current position into the job of your dreams. You can schedule your session by emailing thecareerincubator@cnpstaffing.com

Morgan James
Speakers Group

We connect Morgan James published
authors with live and online events
and audiences who will benefit
from their expertise.